ALLEN COUNTY PUBLIC LIBRARY

P9-ECL-378

ANDY RODDICK

DISCOVER THE LIFE OF A SPORTS STAR II

David and Patricia Armentrout

Rourke
Publishing LLC
Vero Beach, Florida 32964

© 2005 Rourke Publishing LLC

All rights reserved. No part of this book may be reproduced or utilized in any form or by any means, electronic or mechanical including photocopying, recording, or by any information storage and retrieval system without permission in writing from the publisher.

www.rourkepublishing.com

PHOTO CREDITS:
Cover, Pages 5, 21 ©Matthew Stockman/Getty Images; Cover, Page 8 ©Andy Lyons/Getty Images; Title page ©Stan Honda/AFP/Getty Images; Page 19 ©Alex Livesey/Allsport; Page 10 ©Mario Tama/Getty Images; Page 7 ©Ezra Shaw/Allsport; Page 12 ©Gary M. Prior/Getty Images; Pages 14, 15 ©Al Bello/Getty Images; Pages 4, 17 ©Brian Bahr/Getty Images; Page 18 ©Jed Jacobsohn/Getty Images

Title page: *Andy Roddick hugs his trophy after winning the men's final at the 2003 U.S. Open.*

Editor: Frank Sloan

Cover and interior design by Nicola Stratford

Library of Congress Cataloging-in-Publication Data

Armentrout, David, 1962-
  Andy Roddick / David and Patricia Armentrout.
     p. cm. — (Discover the life of a sports star II)
  Includes bibliographical references and index.
  ISBN 1-59515-128-1 (hardcover)
  1. Roddick, Andy, 1982---Juvenile literature. 2. Tennis players--United States--Biography--Juvenile literature. I. Armentrout, Patricia, 1960- II. Title. III. Series: Armentrout, David, ≠ 1962- Discover the life of a sports star II.
  GV994.R63A76 2004
  796.342'092--dc22

2004007613

Printed in the USA

CG/CG

Table of Contents

Andy has become a favorite among young tennis fans.

The One to Watch

There is a new, young face in the tennis spotlight, and it belongs to Andy Roddick. In 2003, at the age of just 21, Andy Roddick became the youngest American since 1973 to finish No. 1 in the history of the **ATP**. Andy Roddick has become the one to watch in men's **professional** tennis!

Full Name:
Andrew Stephen Roddick
Born: August 30, 1982
Residence: Florida and Texas
Plays: Right-handed with a two-handed backhand

Andy's Family

Andy Roddick was born August 30, 1982 in Omaha, Nebraska. His parents, Jerry and Blanche, already had two sons, Lawrence and John.

The Roddick family moved to Texas when Andy was four. When Andy was ten the family moved again, this time to Florida. Andy's parents were seeking better tennis coaching for John.

Relaxing on the beach at Key Biscayne, Florida

Andy takes time to watch tennis action when he is not playing.

Sport-loving Boys

The Roddick boys loved sports. Andy's oldest brother Lawrence was a springboard diver for the U.S. National team. John became an All-American tennis player and is now a tennis coach.

Andy started playing tennis at age seven. He grew up watching John play and worked hard to improve his own game. Andy hit the courts after school and entered junior **tournaments**, even while playing high school basketball.

Andy (left) plays Andre Agassi in an exhibition game in New York during Arthur Ashe Kids' Day.

3 1833 04739 9206

Junior Competition

Andy competed in both singles and doubles junior tournaments. He won seven doubles titles and six singles titles in his junior career.

Andy turned pro in 2000, but since he was only 17 he could still compete at the junior level. In 2000, Andy won junior **Grand Slam** events at the Australian and the U.S. Open. He finished as No. 1 junior in the world.

Andy uses a two-handed backhand to return a shot to Martin Verkerk.

Making the Top 10

Andy did well in his first pro tournaments. In 2000, he became the youngest player (18 years, 3 months) to finish in the top 200.

By the end of 2001, Andy made an incredible jump to finish at No. 16 in the ATP. By the end of 2002 Andy was in the top 10.

Andy's Big Win

Andy had a terrific 2003 season. It began when he made it to the Semi Finals at the Australian Open. He continued to win events throughout the summer. Andy hired coach Brad Gilbert in June, which paid off. Andy ended the season No.1 after winning the U.S. Open. It was Andy's first Grand Slam win as a pro.

Coach Brad Gilbert gets a warm embrace from Andy after his win at the 2003 U.S. Open.

Andy reacts after his first pro Grand Slam win at the 2003 U.S. Open tennis championships.

Rocket Serve

Andy made many improvements to his game his first three years in the pros. He proved he plays well on all surfaces, although hard courts are his favorite. Andy also proved his **serve** is one to be reckoned with. His serves often top 140 miles (225.3 km) an hour. In June of 2003 Andy launched a rocket serve of 149 mph (239.7 kph) that tied the world's record.

Andy follows through on one of his rocket serves!

Andy throws out the first pitch before game 2 of the 2003 Major League Baseball American League division series.

Star Power

Andy's skill and good looks caught media attention and helped him gain celebrity status. He threw out the first pitch at several Major League baseball games. Andy also appeared on several television shows as if he was promoting a new hit movie. Andy was enjoying the attention he brought to men's tennis.

Andy went from number one junior to number one pro in just three years.

Staying Grounded

Andy reached the top of the ranks, but he keeps himself grounded. He stays involved in events that support the Andy Roddick Foundation.

The foundation distributes donated funds to children's charities. The charities help children in many ways. For example, some charities provide needy children with clothing and school supplies. Others help families with children who suffer from illnesses such as cancer. Watch for Andy to continue his winning ways on and off the court.

Andy is presented with a check for the Andy Roddick Foundation during a tennis charity event.

Dates to Remember

1982	Born in Omaha, Nebraska
1989	Starts playing tennis at the age of seven
2000	Ranks No. 1 junior in the world
2000	Turns pro at the age of 17
2001	Finishes in the ATP top 20
2002	Finishes in the ATP top 10
2003	Wins the men's U.S. Open
2003	Ranks No.1 player in the world

Glossary

ATP Association of Tennis Professionals — the governing body of men's professional tennis

Grand Slam (GRAND SLAM) — one of the four major tournaments played once a year: Australian Open, French Open, Wimbledon, U. S. Open

professional (pruh FESH uh nuhl) — a paid instructor or player

serve (SURV) — beginning play by tossing the ball into the air and hitting it with the racket over the net into the service court diagonally opposite; serve is determined by flipping a coin and a player serves for the entire game

tournaments (TUR nuh muhnts) — a series of contests where a number of players try to win the championship

Index

Further Reading

Sadzeck, Tom. *Tennis Skills: The Player's Guide.* Firefly Books, 2001.
Vale, Mark. *Junior Tennis: A Complete Coaching Manual for the Young Tennis Player.* Barrons Education Series, 2002.
Vasquez, Jr.,Reggie. *Tennis For Kids: Over 150 Games to Teach Children the Sport of a Lifetime.* Citadel Trade, 2001.

Websites To Visit

www.usopen.org/
www.atptennis.com
www.andyroddick.com

About The Authors

David and Patricia Armentrout have written many nonfiction books for young readers. They have had several books published for primary school reading. The Armentrouts live in Cincinnati, Ohio, with their two children.